101 ESSENTIAL LISTS
FOR TEACHING ASSISTANTS

101 ESSENTIAL LISTS SERIES

101 ESSENTIAL LISTS
FOR TEACHING
ASSISTANTS

Louise Burnham

continuum
LONDON • NEW YORK

Continuum International Publishing Group
The Tower Building   80 Maiden Lane
11 York Road   Suite 704
London   New York
SE1 7NX   NY 10038

www.continuumbooks.com

British Library Cataloguing-in-Publication Data
A catalogue record for this book is available from the British Library.

ISBN: 0-8264-8872-2 (paperback)

Library of Congress Cataloging-in-Publication Data
A catalog record for this book is available from the Library of Congress.

Typeset by YHT Ltd
Printed and bound in Great Britain by Ashford Colour Press Ltd,
Gosport, Hampshire

CONTENTS

Setting the Scene

LIST 1   What is a teaching assistant?

The term teaching assistant or TA covers a range of roles in a variety of different schools. You could also be known as a:

○ learning support assistant
○ individual support assistant
○ classroom assistant.

As a teaching assistant, you will find that you need to be absolutely clear about what is expected of you. You will be asked to undertake a huge variety of tasks, which makes your job varied and interesting, but you need to be prepared to do them!

Person specification

A person specification defines the personal qualities of the candidate for a particular job. In the case of a teaching assistant it may be extensive. You may not have seen one of these before, but in the advert for your post you might have spotted some of these adjectives. Does this sound like you:

○ flexible
○ adaptable
○ good sense of humour
○ reliable
○ consistent
○ sympathetic
○ calm
○ approachable
○ good communicator
○ respects confidentiality
○ firm but fair
○ positive attitude

- willing to undertake training
- has initiative
- takes an interest in others
- enjoys working with children?

LIST 2

Why be a teaching assistant?

○ You enjoy being with children or adolescents.
○ You experience being part of a strong team.
○ You can work to your own strengths and interests.
○ You will be able to take qualifications and work your way up if you want to.
○ You can be full or part time.
○ You can work around your own children's ages and school hours.
○ You will have long school holidays!
○ You will have an 'insider's' view about the workings of a school.
○ You will experience a true sense of achievement.
○ You will feel as though you are making a real difference to pupils' lives.

LIST 3 Your job description

As the role of the TA has changed so much in recent years, many schools have had to rewrite job descriptions so that they are a more accurate representation of the assistant's responsibilities. In many cases this will mean much more 'individualized' job descriptions. Generally speaking your job description should:

o be made clear to you at interview and you should have a copy when you start your employment
o be a clear and accurate representation of your responsibilities
o be relevant and up to date
o be checked through on an annual basis with your line manager
o outline your role and responsibilities – this may include a 'general' paragraph and then move on to your specific duties
o contain details of the specialized duties of individual support assistants
o possibly include whole-staff responsibilities for issues such as first-aid and school security
o always end with 'and any other duties commensurate with the post' to make sure you can still be asked to do anything!

Your local authority may have devised model job descriptions which match the various levels of qualifications which now exist for teaching assistants.

The National Joint Council for Local Government Services has produced a guidance document which includes several exemplar job descriptions. You can look these up if you go to www.lg-employers.gov.uk.

The changing role of the TA

Are you a teaching assistant, a classroom assistant or a learning support assistant? Although the generic term is teaching assistant, different schools and education authorities may decide to classify different levels of experience by giving assistants different job titles. Expectations have shifted away from simply hearing pupils read and washing paint pots – assistants are now asked to perform a much wider range of duties.

○ You will often take small groups within or outside the classroom, even if your job is really to support an individual child.

○ You may now be asked to take whole classes, although you should not do this unless you have Higher Level Teaching Assistant status.

○ You will need to work on your own initiative, as there is always something to do in a busy classroom! If you're inexperienced and need suggestions, ask your class or subject teacher to leave a notebook of these in a particular place in the classroom so that you can refer to it if he or she is busy. Alternatively, speak to other more experienced assistants to get ideas.

○ Some assistants keep a file in school which will contain class lists, details of any special needs children they are working with, minutes of meetings and any other information which they need to refer to on a regular basis.

○ TAs should have their own information board in the staffroom giving details of meetings, courses and school events.

○ The inclusion of children with special educational needs has also meant that assistants will often need to have quite specialized training. If you are assigned to work with a particular child who has needs which you have little or no experience in managing, do not be afraid to ask your line manager for support and training.

○ In some secondary schools, assistants are working exclusively in specific departments or subject areas in which they are experienced and confident, for example, languages, music or maths. This has meant that they have been able to be more involved with these departments and have closer input in the planning and evaluation process (see List 24 Planning).

Non-teaching tasks

Due to changes in teachers' conditions of service (workforce remodelling), teachers are now no longer required to undertake certain tasks and in many cases these are being delegated to teaching assistants or administrators.

- Collecting money
- Chasing absences
- Bulk photocopying
- Copy typing
- Producing standard letters
- Producing class lists
- Record-keeping and filing
- Putting up classroom displays
- Analysing attendance figures
- Processing examination results
- Collating pupil reports
- Administering work experience
- Administering examinations
- Invigilating examinations
- Administering teacher cover
- ICT troubleshooting and minor repairs
- Commissioning new ICT equipment
- Ordering supplies and equipment
- Stocktaking
- Cataloguing, preparing, issuing and maintaining equipment and materials
- Minuting meetings
- Coordinating and submitting bids
- Seeking and giving personnel advice
- Managing pupil data
- Inputting pupil data.

From DfES *Time for Standards – reforming the school workforce* (DfES, 2002).

Duties and qualifications

The national developments and qualifications framework is designed to provide guidance on the kinds of duties you may be expected to perform according to your experience and qualifications. An inexperienced assistant will be working at Level 1 or Level 2, but someone who has worked in a school for some time will more likely be working at Level 3 or Level 4. Broadly speaking, a Level 2 qualification is equivalent to a GCSE, Level 3 may be likened to an A-level, and Level 4 would be the Higher Level Teaching Assistant (HLTA) status. However, it is important to remember that the HLTA is a status and not a qualification.

To gain a higher level qualification, foundation degrees are now available for teaching assistants. These are usually two-year courses, available through colleges of further education and teacher training colleges.

At each of the four levels you may be supporting and/or delivering learning, and also behaviour management.

Levels of development for teaching assistants

Teaching Assistant Induction/Level 1
Working under direction and instruction of the teacher.

○ Welfare and personal care of pupils
○ Taking small groups or working one-to-one
○ General clerical or organizational support for the teacher.

Teaching Assistant NVQ 2
Working under instruction and guidance.

○ Welfare and personal support – special educational needs (SEN)
○ Delivering pre-determined learning, care and support programmes
○ Implementing literacy and numeracy programmes
○ Assisting with the planning cycle
○ Clerical and administrative support for the teacher or department.

Teaching Assistant NVQ 3 – Specialist Knowledge/Skills
Working under guidance.

○ Involved in the whole planning cycle
○ Implementing work programmes
○ Evaluation and record-keeping
○ Cover supervisor
○ Specialist SEN/subject/other support
○ Pastoral support
○ Learning mentor
○ Behaviour support
○ Exclusions and attendance.

NVQ 4 – Specialism/Higher Level TA/Management responsibilities
Working under an agreed system of supervision/management.

○ Leading the planning cycle under supervision
○ Specialist knowledge resource
○ Delivering lessons to groups and whole classes
○ Management of other staff
○ Pastoral support
○ Mentoring and counselling
○ Behaviour support
○ Exclusions and attendance.

For more on undertaking different qualifications see Chapter 10 Moving On.

LIST 7 — Courses and INSET

As an employed member of staff, you should be invited to in-service training (INSET) and training days. These will:

- usually take place at the beginning or end of term
- be designed to keep all staff up to date with any changes or new requirements as they come into practice
- update current skills
- instruct you on new school policies or procedures.

You may also be invited to courses which are run through your local LEA and should make use of them wherever possible. Examples of these might be:

- behaviour management
- DfES induction for teaching assistants
- counselling for older pupils
- curriculum courses for individual subject areas
- Phonografix training
- training for extra literacy support programmes
- health and safety courses
- school development
- special educational needs
- ICT courses, e.g. SmartBoard training
- restorative justice.

If you get to know assistants in other schools, ask if you can go and work-shadow them to gain an insight into how other schools work. It may be particularly interesting for primary assistants to shadow secondary assistants, or for new assistants to shadow those who are more experienced. Get to know how other assistants manage their time and communicate effectively with teachers and other staff.

LIST 8 Keeping records of continuing professional development

Always keep a record of courses and training you have undertaken – it's easy to forget with the passing of time how much experience and training you have had! If you are lucky your line manager may have done this for you, but you should keep this and update it at least annually. It will also be useful if you apply for a new post, as you will be able to talk about your continuing professional development. Remember to include:

○ title of course
○ date(s) attended
○ where attended
○ name of trainer
○ whether the course is accredited and, if so, confirmation of this, e.g. certificates
○ whether you need to renew the course (e.g. first-aid) and when
○ any useful notes or points to remember from the course.

You may also attend courses alongside other school staff as part of INSET. Do not forget to include these as they are often specific to curriculum subjects or areas of special educational needs and may well be very useful. Often INSET days are optional for support staff, but you should always attend wherever possible as they are usually good for team-building as well as providing an opportunity for additional training. As these often take place on the school premises, you only need to record the date, title of the course and name of the trainer.

Your School

2

LIST 9 Types of school

It is important that you have a good picture of the kind of school you are working in, and what this means, so that you have a clear understanding of the ethos of the school and who it is answerable to. The main categories of school are:

1   Local education authority schools. These are funded by the local authority and may be one of the following:

- community school – the LEA owns the land and buildings, funds the school, employs the staff and provides the support services. The admissions policy is usually determined and administered by the LEA
- voluntary-controlled school – the land and buildings are owned by a voluntary organization, usually a church. The school is funded by the LEA, which employs the staff and provides the support services
- voluntary-aided school – the land and buildings are normally owned by a voluntary organization, usually a church.
- foundation school – the land and buildings are owned by the governing body, which also employs the staff and buys in most of the support services. The admissions policy is determined and administered by the governing body
- special school – some are LEA maintained and can be community, voluntary or foundation schools.

2   Schools not maintained by the local education authority, which include:

- independent schools – funded by fees paid by parents. The headteacher and governing body employ the staff and determine the admissions policy

- City technology colleges – there are a limited number of these. They are non-fee-paying independent schools
- Special schools not maintained by the LEA
- Early-learning organizations.

In most cases the governing body is responsible for the running of the school.

LIST 10 Staff structure and responsibilities

The school will have a defined list of responsibilities for staff which should also indicate how information is passed around the school. Depending on the age group of the pupils and the type of school, the following might be one example:

○ Headteacher, deputy or assistant headteachers, senior managers – responsible for the smooth day-to-day running of the school. The senior management team also reports to the governors on a regular basis.

○ SENCO (special educational needs coordinator) – responsible for all children in the school who have special educational needs. This includes keeping paperwork up to date, attending meetings, supporting teachers and arranging for specialist help within and outside school.

○ Year-group leaders – responsible for coordinating teachers in the same year group.

○ Subject leaders – responsible for managing their subject across the school. This includes overseeing children's work and making sure that the curriculum is being covered.

○ Class teachers – responsible for registration, pastoral care and support of individual classes.

○ Support staff – schools have a range of support staff, including teaching assistants, administrative staff, midday supervisors and technicians. Each group of staff should meet on a regular basis to ensure that everyone is kept up to date with what is happening in the school.

○ Premises officer – undertakes a wide range of roles and is often also responsible for health and safety within the school.

LIST 11 The governing body

As the school governors have ultimate responsibility for all school matters, it is important to understand a little about their role and how the governing body functions.

You may find that they come to the school to speak to the headteacher or visit classrooms during the daytime, so you will get to know some of them. In general, governing bodies:

○ are responsible for the running of the school
○ consist of around 12–18 people
○ employ the staff
○ hold regular meetings, usually outside school hours
○ include representatives from the school (including support staff) and the community
○ are divided into different committees which meet independently and then report back to the full governing body, usually under the following or similar titles:
  – Curriculum Committee
  – Facilities or Premises Committee
  – Personnel Committee
  – Finance Committee.

You may wish to consider joining the governing body as it gives a valuable insight into how the school is run! For more information on joining and to find out whether there are vacancies, contact your headteacher.

School policies

There is usually an extensive list of these! You should know where your school policies are and how to access them, so that you're aware of school procedures. All policies should be updated on a regular basis and give guidance to staff and parents. Examples of school policies might be:

Curriculum policies

- ○ Subject-specific policies, e.g. mathematics, geography
- ○ Teaching and learning policy
- ○ Planning and assessment policy (including planning with the teacher or how to access the teacher's intentions, feeding back to the teacher, recording information on pupils)
- ○ Assessment, recording and reporting (including marking) policy
- ○ TA involvement in statutory assessment procedures
- ○ Special educational needs policy
- ○ Personal, social and health education policy (includes sex education)
- ○ Early years policy.

Non-curriculum policies

- ○ Anti-bullying policy
- ○ Behaviour management policy
- ○ Child protection policy
- ○ Data protection guidelines
- ○ Drugs awareness policy
- ○ Equal opportunities policy
- ○ Energy and environmental policy
- ○ Finance policy (including purchasing policy, best value statement, write-off and lettings policies)
- ○ Gifted and talented/more able policy
- ○ Health and safety policy
- ○ Homework policy
- ○ Inclusion policy
- ○ Library policy
- ○ Pay policy
- ○ Performance management policy

- Race equality and cultural diversity policy
- School self-evaluation policy.

Your school will probably have its own website which will also provide information about school policy.

Other documentation

It is useful to know the location of these documents. These may be stored centrally, for example in the school office or staffroom.

- The National Curriculum
- The Special Educational Needs Code of Practice 2001
- The locally agreed RE syllabus
- Qualifications and Curriculum Authority (QCA) documents for subject areas
- The school development plan (SDP), sometimes called the institutional development plan
- Long-term and medium-term curriculum plans
- The school prospectus
- Governors' annual report to parents, and governing body minutes
- School circulars and magazines
- Safety booklets for science and D&T
- Instruction booklets for apparatus.

The learning environment

Broadly speaking, the learning environment is anywhere within or outside the school where you take groups or individuals to learn. You are responsible, along with other staff, for making sure the school learning environment is a stimulating place for pupils, so displays and organization of these areas should reflect this. If staff show pride and respect for their surroundings, it will be passed on to pupils.

The learning environment includes:

○ classrooms
○ ICT suite
○ gym or sports hall
○ science labs
○ language labs
○ music room
○ library.

Outside areas:

○ school pond
○ garden
○ playground/field
○ athletics track
○ football/rugby field.

Further afield:

○ areas and sites visited on trips and school journeys. You should remember in this situation that pupils are representing the school and you need to know their whereabouts at all times (and for health and safety reasons)
○ the local area – the church, park or local businesses where pupils may go on work experience.

Extra-curricular activities

It isn't only the curriculum that you support. It can also be very rewarding to get involved with other groups or activities which add to the life of the school.

○ PTA, PSA or PTFA (parent–teacher, parent–staff or parent–teacher and friends association) – this can be responsible for many things, including raising money for the school, selling uniform, organizing parent representatives from different classes or keeping parents informed about issues relating to the school.

○ Out-of-school clubs – these will be activities relating to sport, music or other interests, such as chess, and will usually take place after the school day or during lunch breaks. If you have particular expertise or interest in any of these areas, your support and enthusiasm will be very welcome.

○ Organizing fundraising activities for specific projects, for example, new computer equipment.

○ Helping with administrative or organizational tasks.

○ Helping with special events, such as sports days and school fairs.

LIST 16

Fitting in to your new school

○ When starting at a new school, get to know the names and responsibilities of other staff as soon as possible. Remember this does not only mean teaching and support staff!

○ Make sure you use the correct form of address with other staff and be careful when pupils are close by.

○ Make sure you know who your line manager is and how to contact them if you need to.

○ Take time to speak and listen to others, including pupils!

○ Be careful with your dress. Find out about the school dress code and what is acceptable. Also remember things like low necklines may be fine when standing up straight but not if leaning over and speaking to a small child!

○ Take your cues from others. If there is a staff fund for tea and coffee, for example, make sure you are up to date with any payments.

○ Be supportive of others, make coffee for those who have been on playground duty, check rotas and make sure you are always where you should be. Set yourself reminders if necessary.

○ Keep 'to do' lists and make sure you refer to them!

Educational jargon

Every workplace has its fair share of jargon, and schools are no different. You're bound to come across some of these, so it's worth knowing what they mean.

- ADHD – Attention deficit hyperactivity disorder
- ALS – Additional literacy support
- ASD – Autistic spectrum disorder
- Becta – British Educational Communications and Technology Agency
- BSP – Behaviour support plan
- CoP – Code of Practice
- D&T – Design and technology
- DfES – Department for Education and Skills
- EAL – English as an additional language
- EMAS – Ethnic minority achievement strategy
- FLS – Further literacy support
- HLTA – Higher Level Teaching Assistant
- ICT – Information and communications technology
- IEP – Individual education plan
- LEA – Local education authority
- LSA – Learning support assistant
- NVQ – National Vocational Qualification
- PSHE – Personal, social and health education
- QCA – Qualifications and Curriculum Authority
- SEN – Special educational needs
- SALT – Speech and language therapy
- SATs – Standard assessment tests
- SDP/SIP – School development/improvement plan
- SENCO – Special educational needs coordinator
- SENDA – SEN and Disability Act 2001
- SSA – Special support assistant
- TDA –Training and Development Agency for Schools (formerly Teacher Training Agency).

Working with the Teacher | 3

3

LIST 18 Getting along

You may be permanently in one classroom alongside a class teacher, as in a primary school, or constantly moving between subject areas, as in a secondary school. Although you will always get on with some teachers better than others, remember that all relationships need to be worked at. Your relationship with the teacher is the most important part of what you do.

- Remember you are there to support the teacher – you can each use your energies more productively if you are happy in your role.
- Make sure you ask to see plans wherever possible and read through them beforehand.
- Find out whether you can be involved in planning so that you can make your own suggestions and/or use your expertise. This may involve changing timetables around, but it will be time well spent.
- Be on time – early if you can – so that you are present for the entire lesson, particularly if you have not been able to check through the plan. It will be difficult for both of you if the teacher has to explain tasks more than once.
- If you have something happening at home or outside school which is affecting your work in the classroom, let the teacher know, particularly if you might need to leave the lesson before the end.
- Always speak to the teacher if what you have been asked to do is not clear. Clarify any questions and raise any concerns. This is particularly important if you are supporting a child who has special educational needs, as you may have more understanding of what they can do.
- Check that you have any resources or materials that you need before you go to the lesson.

- Make notes on anything you need to remember to ask the teacher but do not have the time or opportunity to do during the lesson.
- Make sure you have time to discuss any concerns you have afterwards (see also List 25 Feedback).
- Remember to thank the teacher!

LIST 19   **Working with supply teachers**

You may be asked to work alongside a supply teacher with the class or pupil(s) you usually support if the teacher is absent. Often pupils will present a challenge to supply teachers and you will be in the position of knowing what the 'norms' of expected behaviour are. Working with supply teachers can also mean that you are asked, often at the last minute, to undertake duties that are different from those you usually do.

○ Before you start, find out their name, introduce yourself and tell the supply teacher how often you are in that particular class.

○ Make sure you tell the supply teacher about any folders or information books which have been left out for their benefit if this has not been done already.

○ Make sure they know their way around the school, or find a map to help them if they need to change classes.

○ If there is no information readily available, tell them about times of routine parts of the school day, e.g. assemblies, breaktimes, timetabled activities.

○ Talk to them about school rules and sanctions or rewards which normally apply in the classroom.

○ Help with pupils' names! This may be particularly helpful if there are pupils whose names are difficult to remember, such as twins.

○ Give them any information about pupils who have special educational needs or health needs, e.g. pupils with asthma or food allergies.

○ Identify those pupils who may present challenging behaviour and outline any strategies which are usually implemented to prevent this.

○ Inform them about health and safety issues, e.g. who the first-aiders are and what to do in a fire drill.

○ Introduce them to other staff at breaktimes – staffrooms can be lonely places if you don't know anyone!

How to support each other

Both teachers and assistants may need training in order to raise awareness of how best to support each other – only more recently trained teachers may have had training in managing other adults. Assistants who are happy with their teachers say that they feel valued and respected by the teaching staff.

○ Remember that in order to support one another fully, teachers and teaching assistants need to communicate effectively.
○ Remember niceties – thank the teacher.
○ Try not to make assumptions about others.
○ Keep your communication non-verbal if at all possible during teaching time – sometimes gestures or eye contact can speak volumes.
○ Allow as much time for planning and feedback as you can.
○ If you are not invited to staff meetings, ask whether this could be a possibility.
○ Keep up to date with school developments – if you are not told, make a point of asking!

Time management

Effective time management is crucial, especially since teaching assistants are paid by the hour and there is always so much to do! Often teachers say that they do not have time to sit down and plan with assistants, especially in secondary schools. This can be a problem, particularly where pupils need specialist support and tasks may need to be adapted beforehand.

○ Keep lists of what you need to do – carry around a notebook!
○ Speak to teachers you work with and find out whether there are set tasks that they would like you to do each week so that you can get into a routine.
○ Make sure you write down any important points which you need to tell specific members of staff, for example, if you are working with an individual pupil.
○ Check your timetable and see if you can use any pockets of time more productively.
○ Remember to make a point of taking breaks but do not stay over long! Take your cues from others.
○ Be careful not to take too much on, e.g. being a breakfast club, midday or after-school club supervisor, as well as a teaching assistant in a primary school – this cuts down on your communication time with other staff.
○ If your children go to the same school as the one in which you work, try to allow one day a week where they go home with a friend so that you have time to talk to the teachers.
○ Ask for meeting time with your line manager and other assistants at least once a month – it is easier to communicate information to large numbers of people all at once.
○ If you are inexperienced, ask if you can shadow a higher level teaching assistant to see how they manage their time.
○ Show you value others' time by being punctual for lessons and meetings.

LIST 22 **Observing pupils**

You may be asked as part of your role to make observations of specific pupils. Observation can take a variety of forms. We might observe in order to:

○ report to other professionals or to parents
○ resolve a specific problem
○ inform planning
○ evaluate different strategies
○ learn more about a particular pupil
○ see whether pupils are progressing
○ look at a pupil's development, learning and/or behaviour.

Before carrying out an observation, make sure you know what the school's policies are for pupil observations and for confidentiality.

You might be asked to observe:

○ Pupils interacting with one another, to look at:
  – level of social skills
  – language development.
○ Groups of pupils working together, to look at:
  – whether they behave differently in a group
  – whether they can take turns
  – whether they give others opportunities to put forward ideas.
○ Pupils working individually, to look at:
  – how long they can concentrate on an activity
  – whether they are able to work without distractions.
○ A pupil during a whole-class activity or discussion, to look at:
  – whether they are involved and participating
  – whether they take account of the views of others.
○ Pupils working on creative or academic activities, to look at:
  – whether they are confident in expressing their own individuality
  – how they are progressing.
○ Pupils involved in physical activities, to look at:
  – whether the pupil is developing at the same rate as his/her peers
  – whether the pupil is able to carry out physical activities

   – whether the pupil can work as part of a team and how they cope with success and failure.

When you are observing, remember:

- ○ confidentiality
- ○ be objective – only record what you see and hear
- ○ try not to make it obvious that you are observing, if possible.

Record-keeping

As well as observing pupils for assessment purposes, you will come into contact with other kinds of pupil records, for a variety of reasons.

○ School records on pupils, such as:
  – records of any medical conditions or allergies which the child has, doctor's contact details
  – personal contact details and emergency phone numbers.
○ Pupil and class registers.
○ Records of money paid for photographs, school trips, etc.
○ Special educational needs records, including information from outside agencies.
○ Records of schemes of work, plans and assignments.
○ Records from other schools which are sent when pupils transfer.
○ Records of accidents and incidents in school.

If you are asked to complete records, make sure any information you put down is clear and concise. Always store records securely or return them directly to the member of staff who has asked you to complete them.

LIST 24 Planning

Where possible you should always have a copy of the teacher's plan before the lesson. However, in the real world many assistants report that there is no time for this. Some schools have set aside planning time for teachers and assistants to work together, for example during assembly time or lunchtimes. If you do not have any time to talk to teachers beforehand, try and make time later, and ask whether you can see a copy of what they are doing.

- ○ Be pushy! Plans will help you in your role and they should not be a secret, so ask to see copies if they are not readily available, e.g. on the wall of the classroom or staffroom.
- ○ Find out the difference between long-, medium- and short-term planning.
- ○ Make sure the plans specify your role and that of any other staff members in the classroom.
- ○ Check that you understand exactly what you are required to do.
- ○ If you have plans in advance, ask whether you can make your own suggestions – if you are working with an individual pupil, or have a subject specialism your contribution could be valuable.
- ○ Knowing about plans will give you a clearer idea of what is happening and how it fits into the long term.

Feedback

Giving feedback is crucial as it enables the teacher to plan effectively for the next lesson. If you find that you do not have time to feedback verbally to the teacher following the lesson, you will need to find an alternative means. This could be in the form of a specific feedback sheet if necessary. You will need to:

○ include names of all pupils and lessons supported and the date
○ include learning objectives
○ be specific about children with individual education plans, particularly if the work has been related to their targets
○ include context where necessary, e.g. 'John could not concentrate today as he was anxious about taking his swimming badge this afternoon'
○ make sure you give the teacher information about all the pupils you have supported
○ highlight exactly how much the pupil understood and achieved the learning objective
○ include how much encouragement they may have needed to complete the task
○ evaluate the effectiveness of the task.

Working with Others

LIST 26   Relating to others

There are many people within and outside the school with whom you will come into contact in the course of your work. You may be unsure of the role of some of these people, but find out who they are! (See also Chapter 2 for the roles of school staff.) Life will be much easier if you have a good relationship with the whole school community. So, take note of the following:

- You will work better with both pupils and other staff if you take the time to get to know them.
- Take account of other people's circumstances and points of view.
- Pass on colleagues' achievements to others.
- Allow some time for people to take in what you have told them before jumping to conclusions.
- School staff are often very stretched and you may not be the only one with a problem.
- Smile and acknowledge others as a matter of course.
- Make sure you 'actively listen' to others – make eye contact, listen to what they are saying and follow up on things they have told you about.
- Be patient with pupils – they may have difficulty in understanding or acting on what you have asked them to do.
- Remember to act on what you are asked to do – it is awkward to have to repeat instructions to people.
- Remember that very few people get along with everyone!

Other staff within the school

It definitely pays to be on good terms with everyone who works in school – it makes for a better atmosphere if all staff members get on well, and you never know when you might need a favour!

○ Midday supervisors (you may also be one of these!).
○ Cleaners – you may not see cleaners as they will come early or late in the day.
○ Teaching staff – your contact may be limited to those in your particular year group or department.
○ Senior management – make sure you know who these people are and what they do, and not just the headteacher and deputy.
○ Other support staff – office administrators, technicians.
○ Peripatetic teachers – these are specialist teachers who come from off-site, e.g. for music tuition.
○ Premises officers.
○ Contractors, such as gardeners.
○ Governors – you may not have much contact with governors, although support staff will have a representative on the governing body.

You will also probably have, at any one time, student teachers on placements, parent helpers and pupils on work experience. The student teachers will:

○ be in most schools on a regular basis
○ be at different points in gaining their qualification, since most will need to do at least one teaching practice, so some will be more confident than others
○ need to both shadow a teacher and take groups or whole classes for set periods
○ need to manage teaching assistants but may not have been trained in this yet.

The parent helpers and pupils on work experience:

○ will be competent to a lesser or greater degree
○ are almost always very welcome by the school
○ may need some support from you, e.g. finding out about school routines and what is expected of them.

LIST 28 Communication with parents

Whether or not you have contact with parents will vary between schools and roles, and some assistants may be invited to parents' evenings if they support pupils who have special educational needs. In a primary school you may have some contact with parents at the beginning and end of the day, whereas in a secondary school your main form of communication will probably be written.

- If you need to write, make sure you use the preferred form of address, e.g. Mrs Said, Ms Webster.
- Remember, not all children live with their parents and you might be speaking to a carer or grandparent.
- Remember, families now vary enormously from single parents to gay parents and extended families.
- Be aware of cultural differences and wishes.
- Be aware that parents may ask you for advice and you need to know what to do if you are not sure how to help.
- Expect to give to and seek information from parents on a regular basis.
- If you find that there are communication difficulties, for example, if a parent does not speak English, seek help or advice.
- Try to avoid jargon or technical language.
- Ensure you pass on important information straight away, as things can be quickly forgotten.
- Be aware of confidentiality.
- Respect parents' wishes, even if you may not agree with them.
- Take care when handling sensitive situations – ask for help if necessary.
- Share information about the school with parents and involve them as much as possible.

Working with outside agencies

You will almost certainly work with agencies from outside the school, in particular if you support a pupil who has special educational needs. Agency specialists will offer support and advice on specific issues, and help set educational, behavioural and physical targets for pupils.

○ Make sure you know who they are and why they are in school if you are involved.
○ Take time to speak to them in the staffroom if they are on their own, and make them feel welcome.
○ Find out exactly how you can support each other by speaking to them or to the SENCO.
○ Ask about training or read pupils' records or notes if you are supporting pupils who have medical conditions or specific learning difficulties.

Examples of the kinds of agency specialists that you might work with include:

○ physiotherapist
○ occupational therapist
○ speech and language therapist
○ sensory support service
○ school nurse
○ medical specialists
○ complex communications service
○ social services
○ curriculum advisors
○ educational psychologists
○ language support teachers for EAL (English as an additional language) pupils.

LIST 30   Being a team player

You will be a member of several teams, from the whole-school team to perhaps a subject team or year group. As part of the team you are responsible for supporting one another.

○ Remember that the team shares decisions and that your actions must be consistent with these.
○ This is corny, but remember there is no 'I' in 'team'!
○ Make sure you are aware of exactly who everyone is and what their roles are – if you don't know, find out!
○ Accept that for a team to be successful it relies on the skills of a range of personalities.
○ Involve all team members in discussion about important issues.
○ Remember you are there to support each other – do not be anxious about seeking help.
○ Help others out where possible.
○ Be considerate towards others.
○ Do not gossip or speak about other members of the team negatively.
○ Do not let others in the team down.
○ Remain professional at all times.
○ Recognize and applaud the achievements of others in your team.

Attending meetings

LIST 31

You may have always attended staff and school meetings, or it may be a new experience for you. Try to remember the following points.

○ Make sure you are adequately prepared for the meeting and know why you are there.
○ Provide any relevant reports, if requested, before the meeting so that others can read them.
○ Read the agenda beforehand and have some ideas ready.
○ Make sure you are aware of the roles of others.
○ Keep your contributions consistent with your role as a teaching assistant.
○ Don't be afraid of putting your ideas forward, but do not monopolize meetings with your opinions.
○ Express your ideas and thoughts clearly.
○ Remain professional – do not speak negatively about others or their suggestions.
○ Take time to reflect on what has been said and read any minutes or notes.

LIST 32 Managing conflict and facing problems

When working with others it is inevitable that you will face areas of difficulty at some point. This could be anything from contractual details to not getting along with another member of staff, and you will need to know what to do about it and where to go for help.

○ Face up to problems – don't let them stew!
○ Choose who to discuss your problem with carefully, as some people may be more supportive than others.
○ Find a mediator if necessary.
○ Try to avoid dealing with problems inappropriately, e.g. by drinking too much alcohol or coffee.
○ Talk problems through rationally rather than in a confrontational way.
○ Put problems in writing if necessary.
○ Try not to let problems get out of proportion – things are often not as bad as they seem.
○ Make sure you have all the facts.
○ Remember, the most common problems are caused by lack of communication.
○ Check through your school's grievance policy or staff handbook for additional information and help.
○ If necessary, refer to your local education authority or trade union.
○ Make a point of reflecting on and learning from what happens.

What are we Teaching? | 5

LIST 33   Foundation Stage curriculum

From the ages of three to five, that is from nursery to the end of the Reception year, children are taught according to the Foundation curriculum. This is organized into six areas:

1 Personal, social and emotional development
2 Communication, language and literacy
3 Mathematical development
4 Knowledge and understanding of the world
5 Physical development
6 Creative development.

Key points

○ For each of the six areas, pupils are working through 'stepping stones' towards 'early learning goals'.
○ Consideration is given to the fact that children all come from different starting points.
○ What children are learning should be relevant to them.
○ Activities should be 'planned and purposeful' and take place both indoors and outdoors.
○ Pupils will not be taught by 'subject', although at the end of the Foundation Stage they will be assessed by staff under each of the above headings and the information passed to Year 1 teachers.
○ The Foundation Stage focuses on developing children's independence through encouraging them to think for themselves and make their own decisions.
○ There should be an opportunity for children to engage in activities planned by adults, as well as those they initiate themselves.
○ The Foundation Stage document emphasizes the importance of partnerships with parents.

The National Curriculum

The National Curriculum was introduced for the first time in 1988. Until this point, what was taught in schools was not compulsory. The National Curriculum was devised with four purposes in mind:

○ to establish an entitlement to learning for all pupils
○ to establish standards for all subjects
○ to promote continuity and coherence
○ to promote public understanding.

It is divided into four key stages:

○ Key Stage 1 – ages 5–7
○ Key Stage 2 – ages 7–11
○ Key Stage 3 – ages 11–14
○ Key Stage 4 – ages 14–16.

Testing takes place at the end of each key stage against expected levels of attainment in core subjects (English, mathematics and science).

○ You should be able to find copies of curriculum documents in staffrooms, departments or classrooms.
○ Take time to read through and look at the expectations of attainment for the age group you are supporting.
○ Be clear about how the requirements of the National Curriculum fit in with teachers' plans. These will be:
  – long term (annually): a broad outline of topics, areas of study or schemes of work
  – medium term (termly or half termly): more detailed and split into weeks
  – short term (daily): giving learning objectives, group activities and differentiation.
○ Remember that the school curriculum is not just about learning in individual subject areas but covers a broader context, such as pupils relating to others and gaining in self-confidence.
○ Find more information at www.qca.org.uk/232.html and www.curriculumonline.gov.uk (England) and www.accac.org.uk/index_en.php (Wales).

National Curriculum levels

National Curriculum levels are designed to measure pupils' progress in each subject. The levels:

○ are listed under each subject area as attainment targets
○ measure how much pupils know, understand and can do.

Pupils will move up through the levels as they move up through the school but will not all progress at the same rate. At different stages of testing, average attainment levels are as follows:

○ Key Stage 1 – level 2
○ Key Stage 2 – level 4
○ Key Stage 3 – level 5/6
○ National Curriculum targets are not used for assessment at Key Stage 4 as pupils will be undergoing GCSEs.

LIST 36 — Subjects

In primary schools, the National Curriculum is divided into ten subjects:

- English
- Mathematics
- Science
- ICT
- Design and technology
- Art
- Music
- PE
- History
- Geography.

Pupils are also taught personal, social and health education and citizenship, and RE according to the local syllabus. For each of these subjects the QCA (Qualifications and Curriculum Authority) has published suggested schemes of work which schools can adopt if desired. These will be available in most schools and can be found at www.qca.org.uk.

In secondary schools, the National Curriculum includes:

- English
- Mathematics
- Science
- ICT
- Modern foreign languages
- Design and technology
- Art and design
- Music
- PE
- History
- Geography
- Citizenship
- Religious education
- Personal, social and health education
- Careers education
- Work-related learning.

LIST 37
Supporting literacy and numeracy

If you are working in a primary school, you will almost certainly be involved in teaching aspects of the National Literacy or Numeracy Strategies. Secondary schools will follow the National Strategy for Key Stage 3. These are detailed frameworks for the teaching of English and mathematics within the National Curriculum.

○ The Literacy and Numeracy Strategies are designed to raise standards in these areas – you should have seen copies of them and been made aware of the plans which are included for each year group.
○ Look at the strategies and familiarize yourself with how each year group works through the specific plans.
○ The structure and timings of these sessions are outlined in the first section of the strategies – have a look at these as they will help you to understand the sessions.
○ If you are asked to support groups, make sure you are present for the first part of the session or have a clear understanding of what pupils are doing.

Giving extra support

Pupils in Year 1, Year 3 and Year 5 can get extra help with literacy through the early, additional and further literacy support programmes known as ELS, ALS and FLS. For Year 7 pupils there are LPUs (literacy progress units). These are non-statutory but many schools take advantage of them and as a teaching assistant you are likely to be involved with them, although you may need specific training beforehand.

The programmes:

○ are fast paced and intensive
○ are taught in small groups
○ revisit areas which pupils have already covered but need to go over
○ are usually run over a 12-week period during the second term of the school year
○ are designed to help pupils attain national targets for their key stage
○ have specific session plans and resources, provided in a special trolley
○ provide ongoing pupil assessments and regular checks on progress
○ can also be a valuable resource for pupils who have special educational needs or for traveller children who may have missed the original sessions.

LIST 39

Hearing young children read

When supporting young children, you want them to become independent readers and not rely on you. Remember that quite fluent readers may still not have a good understanding of the text. So:

- Try to encourage them as much as possible.
- Talk about the book with them before you start, and discuss what they think it might be about.
- Use all the cues you can, including any pictures – never cover these up!
- Look at initial sounds and try to break words down.
- If their guess makes sense in context and is reasonable, do not necessarily correct them.
- If they are able or older readers, do not correct any mistakes too quickly – encourage them to re-read and self-correct.
- Keep discussing the text with them throughout and ask them to predict the ending if appropriate.
- Ask them to retell the main points of the story or text at the end.

Ideas for remembering spellings

○ Don't let pupils copy unknown words letter by letter.

○ Do help them by asking them to:
  - look at the word
  - say the word
  - cover the word
  - write the word
  - check the word.

○ Check the word together and discuss it. Give praise for correct attempts.

○ For young children, ask them to use the word in a sentence.

○ For older children, ask them to try to think of a mnemonic (a rhyme or phrase) to remember the spelling, e.g. because: **b**ig **e**lephants **c**an **a**lways **u**nderstand **s**mall **e**lephants.

○ Remind pupils of spelling rules, e.g. i before e except after c.

○ Encourage pupils to use dictionaries and vocabulary books or lists.

○ Get pupils to think about the context of the word, and where the word comes from.

○ Say words as they might sound, e.g. parlia-ment, cho-co-late.

○ Find words within words.

○ Think about how you help yourself to remember tricky spellings.

○ Point out the links between words in the same 'family', e.g. definite, finite, infinity.

LIST 41 Strategies for supporting mathematics

○ Encourage pupils to look for mathematics and number in the environment and to see how it impacts on their lives.

○ Use games as much as possible.

○ Devise a 'maths walk' around the school or local area.

○ Remember that language is crucial to understanding and using mathematics:
  - use positional vocabulary (on, over, behind, next to, before, after)
  - encourage pupils to follow sequential directions or instructions
  - use mathematical vocabulary wherever possible in different contexts and draw attention to it
  - encourage pupils to talk about what they are doing as they do it, especially if visualizing or doing mental maths
  - remember that some words used mathematically also have another meaning and that this can be confusing, e.g. table, figure.

○ Make sure pupils use practical examples if they are having difficulties.

○ Help pupils to use open-ended tasks rather than closed ones, e.g. ask 'how many ways can you make 100', rather than giving them straightforward sums.

○ Make sure you are familiar with any resources which you have been asked to use and know where to find them.

Springboard mathematics

Springboard mathematics is the name given to additional catch-up programmes for pupils who need a little extra help with mathematics to achieve at the same level as their peers. They are the numeracy equivalent of the literacy progress units (LPUs).

Springboard mathematics:

○ is designed to help pupils in Years 3, 4, 5 and 7
○ is delivered in the autumn and spring terms
○ is designed to complement the National Numeracy Strategy and is linked to its units of work
○ focuses on number
○ provides support for small groups of children outside the normal numeracy session
○ goes over some of the teaching objectives from the previous year
○ includes detailed teaching points, vocabulary and resources
○ should enable pupils to benefit more fully from the teaching programmes in their year group.

Care is needed when delivering these programmes, particularly if these are the same pupils who are having extra support for literacy. You will need to take pupils' other commitments into account so as not to overwhelm them.

Supporting ICT

ICT is one of the hardest subjects to teach pupils from Reception to Year 11 – and beyond! This is because there will always be pupils of very different abilities, as well as all the technical things which can go wrong. These can include:

○ being unable to turn on or log on to machines
○ problems remembering passwords
○ problems when loading software
○ difficulties with accessories, such as printers
○ machines freezing and pupils having to start again.

You can be more prepared for this by:

○ setting up before you start
○ taking pupils' passwords with you or additional work for them to do if passwords are confidential and they forget theirs
○ making sure you are familiar with computers and programs before using them
○ taking time to check that there is enough ink, that all machines are connected, and you know which computer is attached to the smartscreen, etc.
○ having a back-up plan to use as a last resort!

You will hopefully not be the only adult in the room, or you will only have a small group to manage and not need to be in too many places at once!

You will often have to modify or change tasks that you have been asked to do with pupils. This may be because:

○ pupils find the task too easy or difficult
○ pupils finish the task and you need to fill some time
○ you do not have time to complete the task
○ you want to check that pupils have understood and need to give them a fresh activity.

If so:

○ speak to the teacher about the kinds of things you may be free to do with pupils who have finished their work
○ try and use any areas of expertise you have in particular subjects, such as art or music. Make sure teachers are aware of your strengths, particularly if you wish to develop them
○ always use any spare time you have if you are working with a small group – they may not often have the opportunity to work closely with an adult.

Managing resources

Whatever level you work at as a TA you will have some responsibility for managing and preparing resources. You may be assigned to a subject area, work with a specific member of staff or be responsible for managing stock.

○ Make sure you have a system for tracking what is in school, what is on order and how others should report what is needed.

○ Find out which resources are kept where – items for different subjects will be kept separately from general stock.

○ Write things down as and when you run out of them or you will forget!

○ Try to be as economical as you can when using resources, e.g. when using coloured paper, cut from the edge rather than the middle.

○ Always report any broken or missing items.

○ Only take what you intend to use.

○ Keep resource areas tidy and leave them as you would like to find them.

LIST 46 **Tips for putting up displays**

○ Be constantly on the look out for new ideas for displaying pupils' work – when you find them, either write them down or try them out!

○ Be careful when mounting work – line up your borders so that they are straight otherwise your whole display will look crooked!

○ Pin displays before you commit to stapling them to make sure things are lined up and spaced correctly.

○ Label displays with questions and information so that they hold people's interest.

○ Visit other classrooms in the school from time to time with the sole purpose of looking at what other people do.

○ Don't be afraid of using interactive displays – a table or unit in front of a display board which has items that pupils can handle or look at closely (a bit like a 'nature table') can be very effective. But don't become agitated when pupils actually use it!

○ Never take down an old display unless you have a new one to put up in its place straight away – better an old display than no display!

○ Recycle displays around the school! If you have had a particularly effective display in a classroom which you think others might like to see, ask if it can be moved to a more central area, such as a hall or corridor.

○ Use three-dimensional designs wherever you can – this does not have to be over adventurous but will make the display more effective.

○ Keep an eye on displays you have put up and restaple or glue any areas which start to look 'tired'.

○ Make sure displays in young children's classrooms are not too high for small people to see.

○ Ensure all pupils' work is represented and not always just the 'best' – this is important for pupils' self-esteem.

○ Make sure pupils' names are visible on their work.

LIST 47

Useful things to keep with you

If you are moving around the school and do not work in one classroom or department, you may find it useful to have a bag or box of handy items. What is in your bag will depend on the age of the pupils you support and whether you support a particular subject.

Examples of the kind of items you might need include:

- dry whiteboard markers
- coloured pens and pencils
- red or black biro
- spare paper
- eraser
- sharpener
- ink eraser
- scissors
- glue
- tissues
- extra work, games or ideas
- additional lesson plans
- mathematics kit (compasses, ruler, protractor).

Make a point of naming these items where possible as they may have a tendency to disappear!

Managing Pupils

LIST 48 Working with individual pupils

- Get to know your pupil.
- Find out about their background and what makes them tick.
- If you can, find out their individual learning style (see List 49 Individual learning styles).
- Ask for training on any special educational needs or medical conditions the pupil might have.
- Make sure you have the time and resources to carry out the specific work you are asked to do.
- Make sure you know the pupil's targets and other information in their individual education plan (IEP). This could be:
  - educational targets, e.g. to be able to recognize and count numbers to ten
  - behaviour targets, e.g. to keep breaktimes quiet
  - language targets, e.g. to know and recognize core words
  - how the targets are to be implemented and the resources you might need
  - the stage they are at e.g. School or Early Years Action, School or Early Years Action Plus or statement (see List 58 School Action and Statements of SEN)
  - how long they have had an IEP
  - when the IEP is due to be reviewed.
- Keep a positive attitude and transmit this to the pupil.
- Take time to talk to the pupil and listen to them – not only does it make sense, it will also make your job easier!
- Do not be afraid to ask for help!

Individual learning styles

Individual learning styles are an individual's preference for learning about the world. If you find out about the individual styles of pupils it may help you to support their learning. Have a look at www.chaminade.org/inspire/learnstl.htm to find a questionnaire on learning styles which will help you to discover which your style is and enable you to help pupils to find theirs!

Examples of individual learning styles include:

○ visual/spatial – the individual will be able to visualize an object and create mental images
○ verbal/linguistic – these individuals acquire and process knowledge by listening, reading and writing
○ logical/mathematical – this is the ability to think logically and sequentially and reason deductively. These learners will be organized
○ bodily/kinaesthetic – those who learn in this way will be more likely to learn things in a practical way
○ musical/rhythmical – these people may find it easier to learn if they retain information while listening to music or rhythms
○ interpersonal – these will be good communicators and relate well to others
○ intrapersonal – these individuals will be reflective and analytical. They will learn better through independent study and research.

Working with groups

- Find out whether your group of pupils has worked together before or if this is the first time. This is because you will need to:
  - find out some background on what they have done before
  - know how well they work together
  - be clear with them what the ground rules are when working as a group.
- Make sure you are clear on exactly what you have to do with the group – is it a group task or will they be working on individual activities and just sitting together?
- Try not to work with groups of more than six pupils – this will be easier to manage.
- If you are working with children who have special educational needs, make sure your group is as small as possible.
- Sit pupils apart from the start if you know they do not work well together.
- Tell the group the learning objective.
- Make sure you involve all pupils, particularly the quieter ones.
- Do not let the louder or more boisterous pupils have all the ideas and opportunities.
- Report any problems or disruption to the teacher immediately.

Working with different age groups

You may be working with the same age group all the time, for example, where you are attached to a particular class or pupil, or you may move between different classes and ages. With all age groups you will need to establish mutual trust and respect.

○ If you are moving around a lot, take time to think about how you will approach learning with this age group. As a rough guide:

– younger children (nursery and infant) cannot concentrate for long periods. They may seek reassurance and copy adults and other children

– as children become older they will be able to concentrate for longer, although they may still easily be distracted, depending on the level of interest the activity holds

– by secondary school age, pupils will be able to work for longer on tasks for a given time.

○ You may need to focus on social skills as well as academic ability!

○ Make sure furniture and equipment is the right size for the pupils. It can make a real difference to how they manage the activity if, for example, the chairs are the incorrect height for the table or there are inappropriate resources and equipment.

○ Pupils of all ages need plenty of praise! Notice when they do well or try hard and comment on it.

○ Sometimes in a class you will have a child who is much taller or shorter than the rest of the group – try to remember their needs.

○ If you have a group of pupils from different age groups who are working together, watch them carefully to ensure the work is set at an appropriate level for all.

LIST 52   Strategies for supporting pupils

Always have some strategies up your sleeve when supporting pupils to ensure that you are one step ahead! You will also need to have a variety of ideas to keep them focused, as what works one day will not necessarily work the next. Remember to keep up the pace during the lesson you are supporting and involve all pupils.

- ○ Make use of body language – ensure you appear interested and are not 'somewhere else'.
- ○ Make eye contact when speaking to pupils.
- ○ Open-ended questions will always extract more information from pupils – so remember to use them:
  - – what did you do?
  - – how could you have done that differently?
  - – why do you think that happened?
- ○ Provide pupils with a commentary on what is going on – describe what is happening. This will enable them to internalize events and remember any new vocabulary.
- ○ Ask pupils to tell you what they are doing – ask how, what, why.
- ○ Praise and encourage pupils all the time and notice when they get it right – some adults only notice when they get it wrong.
- ○ Remember to tie in the learning objective to what they are doing, e.g. 'Now who can tell me what I needed to remember about capital letters?'
- ○ It is sometimes hard to remember to do this, but check on what they have learned at the end of an activity and challenge them. Ask how it has it changed their thinking. Ask them if there are any 'fuzzy bits' that they are not sure about which you can clarify. This will end the session more effectively.

What is assessment?

While you are supporting learners you are also assessing what they are doing and whether or not they are achieving the learning objective. Assessment is necessary as it gives a breakdown of individual pupils' progress over time and can be used to help with planning.

There are two main types of assessment used in school – formative and summative. Formative assessment:

○ is the ongoing monitoring of pupils' work, which is the main area with which assistants may be involved
○ is classroom based
○ considers how pupils learn
○ provides effective feedback to pupils.

Summative assessment:

○ takes place at the end of a period such as a school year
○ looks at attainment at a particular point in time.

Pupils will also be tracked to make sure that they are meeting targets which have been set by teachers in line with individual expectations. You need to make sure you take note of the level of work achieved by all pupils.

LIST 54 Encouraging independence

An important part of what you do as a teaching assistant is to encourage and help pupils of any age to become as independent as possible.

○ You will often be asked for help by pupils and wherever you can, encourage them to have a go themselves first.

○ Remember your role is as an enabler – you are not there to do the pupils' work for them!

○ If pupils ask you for help, question them about what they have done and what they think they should do next.

○ Try and think of ways of working with pupils that mean they have to think and act independently.

○ Where possible, provide opportunities for them to take on a bit of extra responsibility – helping to set up resources, taking messages, etc.

○ Train pupils to become confident in putting their ideas forward.

LIST 55

Overcoming problems

As you gain more experience in the classroom, you will be more able to deal with challenging behaviour and difficult situations without involving other staff. However, if you ever feel out of your depth when working with pupils you should abandon the activity and speak to another member of staff.

Remember that such problems can be caused by a number of factors, most of which you will have no control over. . . .

- Tiredness
- Illness
- Medication
- Hunger
- Bullying
- Change in routine
- Excitement (end of term/holiday/birthday party/school trip)
- Friendship dynamics
- Moving home
- Bereavement
- Divorce or separation of parents
- Problems within a step-family
- Splitting up with a boyfriend or girlfriend
- Pregnancy or abortion
- Drug, substance or alcohol abuse
- Neglect.

Depending on what the problem is, you should:

- always be in control – you are the adult
- ask the pupil whether they are able to continue with the activity
- be clear with pupils about what you want them to do
- be firm but fair
- make sure you carry out any threats you make
- send for another adult if necessary
- ensure that any intervention you make between pupils is calm and sensible (see Chapter 7 Behaviour Management).

LIST 56   Supporting pupils with special educational needs

You may be working as a learning support assistant (LSA) to support a pupil who has special educational needs. Before you start working with the pupil, you should:

○ ask for as much information as you can concerning the pupil you are supporting, such as:
  - background
  - behaviour
  - how long they have had support
  - parental involvement
  - outside agencies involved
○ go and meet the pupil before the day you start working with them if possible
○ ask the SENCO for help if you need it
○ make sure you are trained and know about the pupil's needs
○ ask to be involved when the individual education plan is being drawn up so that you can have some input
○ know about the pupil's targets and what you both need to work on.

If you have had your time allocated to more than one pupil with SEN, make sure you have time to do the necessary preparation and attend meetings for each child.

LIST 57 Some common special educational needs

In the course of your career you will meet many pupils who have special educational needs. Remember that every child is unique and individual and it is important not to 'label' pupils. This is intended as a rough guide only.

- ADHD – attention deficit hyperactivity disorder is three to four times more common in boys. The ADHD pupil will be unable to concentrate and can be disruptive, having a poor performance at school when compared with intelligence. They will be impulsive, restless and can become frustrated. There are different degrees of severity.

- Autism – this is a neurological disorder which has had a high media profile due to its supposed link to the MMR vaccine. It is also more common in boys than girls. Autistic people have difficulty in the areas of communication, socialisation and imagination. They will sometimes have obsessive interests, for example in computers or trains, and some will also have severe or moderate learning difficulties. Again, the condition may vary in its severity.

- Dyslexia – this is a difficulty in learning to read, write and spell. It affects about ten per cent of the population and can largely be overcome through specialized teaching and use of a variety of strategies. Those supporting dyslexic pupils should have appropriate training.

- Dyspraxia – this is a difficulty in planning and carrying out physical movements. It has an effect on the presentation and organization of work. People with dyspraxia are often said to be clumsy and have a tendency to drop things or have difficulties in judging height or distance.

- Speech and language disorders – these are difficulties in communication and oral motor skills. This may simply be due to immaturity but can be caused by neurological disorders or physical impairment.

- Learning difficulties – this means that pupils are not progressing at the same rate as their peers and may need specific support.

- Physical or sensory disabilities which may impact on pupils' learning – these may be visual or auditory impairments, or fine or gross motor difficulties. Pupils will need support specific to their needs.

School Action and statements of SEN

When a pupil is identified as having a special educational need, there are several stages of monitoring and support that take place, which can lead to the pupil having a statement of special educational needs and appropriate provision funded. The statementing process is usually quite slow and the school has to gather a great deal of evidence and paperwork from different sources in order to request a statement. As a rough guide, the stages are as follows:

- ○ Staff report to the SENCO that the pupil is a cause for concern and the pupil is then monitored.

- ○ The pupil is put on the school's special educational needs register and an individual education plan (IEP) is drawn up, with targets to be worked on during a set timescale. At this stage the pupil is said to be on School Action.

- ○ If during this stage the pupil shows no sign of improvement over two or more terms, the SENCO may decide to involve outside agencies after consulting with parents or carers – this is known as School Action Plus.

- ○ The outside agency or agencies will assist the school in drawing up new targets through work they are implementing with the pupil. This will again be reviewed after a set period and if the pupil still needs further support, the school may apply for a statement.

- ○ All the agencies working with the child, the parents and the school (assistants, teacher, SENCO, headteacher) are asked to write reports giving reasons why the local education authority (LEA) should fund further support for the pupil. This is then sent to the LEA which meets regularly to look at paperwork for pupils who have applied for a statement. The application may or may not be successful. If not, the school may re-apply at a later date.

- ○ Some or all of these stages may be bypassed if it is clear that a pupil will not be able to attend mainstream school without support.

LIST 59 — Working with bilingual pupils

Bilingual pupils will come from a variety of backgrounds and may not have had as much experience of school as other pupils in the class. English may not be their first language or they may be equally fluent in English and another language.

- ○ Remember, lack of competence in English does not automatically mean that the pupil has a learning difficulty.
- ○ Make sure other staff and pupils who have contact with the pupil are aware, particularly if the pupil speaks no English.
- ○ Find additional strategies for developing language skills, or find out about what support is available to help the pupil.
- ○ Find out about resources which are available, e.g. dual language texts.
- ○ Group the pupil with those of a similar ability, not with those who have special educational needs.
- ○ Use strategies which will develop self-esteem and confidence.
- ○ Treat the ability to speak more than one language as a gift!
- ○ Notice when pupils are making progress!

L I S T 60 Managing whole classes

You should not be expected to take a whole class on your own unless you are an experienced teaching assistant or have HLTA status.

○ If you are asked to take a whole class, remember you should be given tasks or a plan by a teacher – if not, ask for one!
○ If you have not taken a whole class before, find out the name of a supportive adult who will be working close by so that you can call on them if necessary.
○ Find out about any pupils who have additional educational needs.
○ Ask whether there will be any other adults in the room for you to manage, such as learning support assistants.
○ Make sure you have all the resources you need before the lesson.
○ You should not take whole classes long term or at short notice without having time to prepare.
○ Ask for additional training if you feel you need it.

LIST 61 Class teaching tips

o Make sure you have the attention of all the pupils before you start speaking.

o Be clear about learning objectives.

o Ensure all pupils have access to and understand how to use any resources.

o Use visual stimuli for clarification if you can.

o Use a variety of strategies, such as questioning, discussing, games and practical examples, to aid understanding.

o Make sure you ask pupils if they have any questions before they start.

o Do not always expect pupils to work in complete silence – sometimes they may need to discuss things with a partner, for example.

o Go over with pupils what they have learned at the end of the session.

LIST 62

Marking work

○ Check with the teacher that he or she is happy for you to mark pupils' work before doing so.

○ Make sure you know and understand the school's marking policy – using red pen, initialling what you have marked – to ensure consistency of approach among staff.

○ Ask whether you can mark the pupils' work when they are with you, if possible, to discuss any issues with them straight away.

○ If you are unable to mark work with pupils, mark it afterwards as soon as possible – pupils need prompt feedback. It does not give them a good message if the work is handed back to them a week or more later.

○ Check whether you should write any comments, e.g. that the pupil was supported doing the work.

Playtime duties

As an assistant, you may be asked to go on playground duty, particularly if you work in a primary school and more staff are needed.

○ Check rotas and remind yourself of your 'duty day'!
○ Swap with other members of staff if you are unable to go out on your day.
○ Make sure you are outside promptly, at the beginning of the break, so that there is an adult on duty immediately.
○ If it is a 'wet play', you may be asked to patrol more than one classroom or supervise children in a hall or other central area – if you are at a new school and are unsure, ask!
○ Avoid taking hot drinks outside if at all possible – pupils will be running around and it is a real health and safety hazard.
○ Avoid chatting to other staff while you are on duty as you are unlikely to be watching pupils' behaviour.
○ Have some games or equipment you can use if necessary.
○ If pupils wish to play football, try to allocate a particular area so that this does not interfere with others.
○ Make sure you know to whom you should report any incidents and where the first-aiders are.
○ Ensure you are not the only one on duty, particularly if it is a large playground which may have areas which are not visible, i.e. behind buildings or sheds.

LIST 64   School trips

These can be fun, interesting or just plain stressful! If you are asked to help with a school trip, find out how many pupils you will need to supervise and get to know them a little beforehand if you don't already. If you have never been to the site before, find out what you can about it.

- ○ Before you go, check money has been handed in and parental consent given.
- ○ Ensure that any pupils with special educational needs will be able to participate in all activities.
- ○ The level of supervision you give will depend on the age of the pupils – remember that young children will be very excitable and will tire easily.
- ○ Make sure you or someone else has a charged mobile phone with them.
- ○ Take contact numbers for parents in case of emergency.
- ○ Take a first-aid kit and any medical equipment, such as inhalers, with you.
- ○ Make sure someone has tissues, sick bags, etc.
- ○ Speak to your group about safety issues, expectations and what will happen if they misbehave.
- ○ Make sure all pupils have any worksheets or questionnaires with them.
- ○ Take spare pens or pencils for those who forget.

Coping with Christmas

Love it or loathe it, Christmas comes around with predictable regularity! You may enjoy the run up to Christmas in school or find it difficult – whichever way you look at it, though, it's always exhausting and you need to be organized.

○ Keep a 'Christmas list' and refer to it in November – Christmas always comes earlier in school! This will remind you of all the things which need to be done between now and the end of term.
○ Make sure you have some Christmas activities or ideas up your sleeve which are appropriate to the age group you support – you may be asked to take more classes or groups than usual at this time of year while there are rehearsals, etc.
○ Pupils might have additional activities such as Christmas worksheets, word searches, games, quizzes, videos or other activities. Make sure you keep those which work!
○ If you have a particular talent for art, music or other subject areas which might be useful for Christmas productions, make sure you tell someone about it.
○ Keep examples of cards, calendars, poems, songs or other items which you have to make each year to remind you what you have done, and store them with others from Easter, Divali and Eid.
○ Try to clear away all evidence of Christmas before you break up – it isn't fun coming back to it in January.

Behaviour Management 7

Why do pupils misbehave?

Most disruptive or anti-social behaviours will have an underlying cause. These can be numerous but may include:

- low self-esteem
- problems at home or with friendships
- insecurity and a need to be noticed
- low expectations of behaviour from adults
- special educational needs which have not been picked up
- inappropriate work for the pupil
- difference in expected codes of behaviour between home and school
- staff attitudes or reactions.

Pupils' behaviour is often a 'self-fulfilling prophesy', in other words, pupils will act in the way that they perceive is expected of them. If we think that Ramona will act up in the lesson, she probably will. Also, what we practise we become good at, so those who habitually misbehave will become better at it. So, when it comes to handling poor behaviour in the classroom, start as you mean to go on.

- Have high (but realistic) expectations for behaviour and make these clear to pupils from day one – it's far easier to start off being a little sterner and relax later than vice versa!
- Follow routines as much as possible. This gives pupils boundaries and makes them feel more secure in the learning environment.
- Make sure pupils know what to do when you set them a piece of work, when they are expected to complete it and what to do if they finish it early.

LIST 67   The behaviour policy

Read your school's behaviour policy and make sure you know what is expected of all staff and pupils. A behaviour policy should give aims and guidelines for effective whole-school behaviour management.

○ School, class or department rules for behaviour can vary depending on where you work:
  - in an infant classroom, you may have a small set of school rules for the children to follow and understand
  - in a junior classroom, you may devise class rules with the children so that they have some say in what is expected in their classroom
  - in a secondary school, rules may be departmental, for example what is expected in an ICT suite or science lab.
○ Care should be taken when setting rules. There should not be too many of them and they should not be too hard to remember.
○ Pupils should be involved where possible when drawing up or revising rules so that they have ownership of them.
○ Rules should be discussed regularly during class and assembly times and displayed so that all pupils are aware of them.
○ Pupils should be clear that if they break the rules the consequences are a result of their actions and it is their choice. Similarly, if their behaviour is good, this should also be noticed.
○ Rules should not be written in a negative way, e.g. 'Do not. ...' as this will lower expectations of pupils. Better to state 'I will. ...' or 'In school we...'
○ Make sure you know the limitations of your role as a teaching assistant when managing behaviour:
  - send for other staff if you need help
  - be aware of the school or local policy on pupil restraint
  - refer to senior management in more serious cases.
○ Remember, consistency between staff is vital! Everyone needs to be aware of what behaviour is expected and what will happen if rules are broken (see List 71 Sanctions).
○ Be aware of factors that will have an impact on pupil behaviour, such as end-of-term excitement or social activities outside school.
○ Be aware of which school policies influence behaviour management within the school, such as those on child protection, anti-bullying, equal opportunities, drugs and health and safety.

LIST 68   Strategies for managing behaviour

- ○ Make sure you know what the school or class strategies are.
- ○ Always follow up important issues – if you tell a pupil you will be speaking to another member of staff about their behaviour, don't forget to do so.
- ○ Try to focus on the behaviour and don't criticize the pupil.
- ○ Keep the focus on primary behaviours. Do not be distracted by what pupils say, e.g. 'I shouted at her but she started it, why aren't you telling her off?' This could draw you into an argument which takes the focus off the original issue.
- ○ Praise work and behaviour genuinely and frequently to reinforce good behaviour and build self-esteem.
- ○ Model the behaviour that you want to see in school – if you spend assembly speaking to the member of staff next to you, you cannot expect pupils to respect you or respond to you if you tell them off for speaking to their friends during assembly. Pupils will mimic negative as well as positive behaviour.
- ○ Remain calm and controlled when dealing with conflict.
- ○ Make sure you follow up on any behaviour management you have had to do by revisiting the pupil later and commenting positively on what they are doing now. It is important to 'catch them being good' and comment on it.
- ○ Use humour if you feel it can diffuse the situation but be aware that it will not work with all pupils.
- ○ Use posters and displays which encourage positive thoughts and self-esteem.

LIST 69   Dealing with bullies

Bullying occurs in both primary and secondary schools. It is persistent and results in pain and distress to the victim. It can be:

- emotional – being unfriendly, excluding, tormenting, e.g. hiding possessions, using threats
- physical – pushing, kicking, hitting or any form of violence
- racist – racial taunts or gestures
- sexual – unwanted physical contact
- verbal – name-calling, sarcasm, spreading rumours, teasing.

Signs of bullying can include:

- a pupil, normally happy at school, loses their enthusiasm
- a pupil's possessions are constantly broken or lost
- academic work declines
- a pupil becomes withdrawn and not themselves, without explanation.

What you can do

- Make sure you establish the facts by speaking to all concerned.
- Support the victim of the bullying and reassure them.
- Reprimand the bully and tell them why their actions are wrong.
- If a pupil is repeatedly involved in bullying, check that the class teacher, headteacher and SENCO are informed.
- Make sure the pupil's parents are informed.
- Read your school's anti-bullying policy for more information on dealing with bullying.

L I S T 70   Building positive relationships with pupils

○ Get to know the pupils you work with. If you are an individual support assistant, you will know exactly what your pupil is capable of and when they are having good or bad days. You will need to vary your interactions with pupils depending on their own personalities and interests.

○ Make a point of building trust with pupils so that they respect you. Pupils will achieve more in a trusting and positive environment. You will find this harder with some pupils than others, especially those who have not always had positive experiences.

○ Take time to get to know a pupil's circumstances and interests. Build up your relationship and show the pupil that you care about them, but be aware that this will take time.

○ Praise good behaviour so that you build self-esteem and foster mutual respect.

○ With younger pupils, where possible, ignore mild, inappropriate behaviour but notice and comment on the good behaviour of others.

○ Be a good listener – listen to all sides and do not get drawn into arguments. Speak to pupils quietly or privately about their behaviour.

○ Use positive language wherever possible. 'Don't run in the corridor' becomes 'We always walk quietly around the school', 'Stop pushing in' becomes 'Line up sensibly'. Positive language is very effective; use it to describe the outcome you want to see rather than commenting or focusing on what you want to stop.

LIST 71 **Sanctions**

Get to know your school policy on sanctions – is there a scale which you need to know about? For example:

○ verbal warning and reminder
○ name on board
○ name written on behaviour card
○ name written on behaviour card three times = miss breaktime
○ name written on card five times = sent to head of year/deputy
○ name written on card eight times = letter sent to parents.

Further examples of sanctions might be:

○ gestures, frowns and eye contact
○ time out
○ moving pupils
○ removing privileges
○ detention
○ reports to other staff.

Applying sanctions

○ Think about how the sanctions apply to the school rules or expectations of behaviour.
○ Make sure you are clear on whether you are free to apply sanctions or whether you need to inform a teacher first – schools will vary in this.
○ Always separate the behaviour from the pupil, e.g. 'That was a very rude thing to say', rather than 'You are being very rude again today, Harry'. This allows the pupil to be redirected rather than lowering self-esteem and expectations of behaviour.

LIST 72 Things to avoid

○ Confrontation – this will not help the situation but will make the pupil defensive.

○ Anger – again, this will make the situation worse. Better to stay calm and speak quietly to the pupil. Tell them you will speak to them later if necessary.

○ Allowing the situation to escalate – get in quickly.

○ Accusations, e.g. 'Did you call out just then?' Open-ended questions are better, such as 'Can you tell me what just happened?'

○ Apportioning blame without having all the details – make sure you ask all pupils what they know.

○ Broadcasting the problem – try to sort out the situation without doing this. It will give the pupil the attention they are craving.

○ Arguing with pupils – it is better to name the behaviour and apply the consequences.

○ Stereotyping, e.g. expecting that boys are more likely to misbehave than girls.

The importance of praise

Praise is a very powerful tool that can help you build good relationships with pupils.

○ Make sure you remember to praise pupils – try to give six positives for every one negative. If you have children of your own, try practising at home and see what a difference it makes!

○ Pupils tend to remember negative comments and dwell on them – think about incidents in your own childhood.

○ Think about how you feel as an adult when your achievements are recognized.

○ Look at other people's use of praise and the difference it makes to pupils' behaviour.

○ Make sure pupils are praised for efforts and not just achievements.

○ Pay particular attention to pupils who find learning difficult.

LIST 74   Rewards

It is important to know about rewarding the pupils you are supporting. School policies will differ and you will need to know what rewards are given and who usually gives them. Depending on the age of the pupils, rewards will vary.

Infants

- smiley faces drawn on good work
- stickers
- gestures such as a smile or a thumbs-up
- choosing a favourite activity
- some staff still give edible rewards but be careful with sweets or cakes, as many children now have food allergies or are unable to have any kind of food without parental consent.

Juniors

- merit marks
- badges
- working towards group rewards
- videos – popular rewards but care should be taken with the choice of film
- sending to a member of staff who knows them for extra recognition of their achievements.

Secondary school

- merit marks
- stamps towards class/house points
- special privileges, such as being first in queue
- classes or groups may also devise their own rules which are known by all members.

Understanding Legislation 8

LIST 75 Keeping up to date

Education is an area which is constantly under scrutiny and it is important to keep up to date with changes in the law and in requirements. The best way of doing this is to read educational publications on a regular basis. Examples of these might be:

- ❍ *The Times Educational Supplement*
- ❍ The *Guardian* education section
- ❍ *Child Education* (Scholastic)
- ❍ *Junior Education* (Scholastic)
- ❍ *Special Children* (Questions Publishing)
- ❍ *Special!* (NASEN)
- ❍ *5 to 7 Educator* (MA Education)

You should also check the appropriate educational websites (see List 101 Useful websites) for the latest developments. Teachers' TV is also of interest and occasionally shows specialized programmes for teaching assistants or relating to areas of special educational need. Make sure you understand the latest jargon and 'buzz words' and know how any new legislation will impact on your role as a teaching assistant.

SEN and Disability Act

Since January 2002, schools have been required to follow the Special Educational Needs Code of Practice which is linked to the Disability Discrimination Act (DDA) 2001. Together, the Code of Practice and the DDA provide a joint approach for ensuring that children with special educational needs (SEN) have their needs met in mainstream schools. This means that:

○ children with SEN have stronger rights to be educated in mainstream schools
○ LEAs must arrange for pupils with SEN to be provided with services offering advice and information
○ schools must inform parents if their child is having special educational provision and treat the parents as partners
○ pupils are consulted about issues and their views are taken into account
○ separate guidance is provided for early years, primary and secondary phases.

The Disability Discrimination Act was introduced to prevent employers from treating disabled workers less favourably than others. It was amended in 2001 to include schools and to prohibit discrimination against disabled children. This means that schools now have to:

○ plan for and make progress in improving the physical environment for disabled children at school
○ ensure that any new buildings or provision have suitable entrances, toilet facilities, etc.
○ make sure that disabled pupils are not placed at a disadvantage compared to other pupils.

Understanding inclusion

Since the 2001 SEN Code of Practice came into force, the term 'inclusion' has been used where before we might have talked about equal opportunities. Inclusion means that:

○ there should not be discrimination of any kind within schools
○ pupils should not have to be segregated from their peers to achieve adequate educational provision

○ all pupils should have access to the full range of educational opportunities provided
○ all staff should be aware of pupils who have specific needs
○ stereotyping and prejudice should be challenged wherever they occur
○ diversity should be celebrated and all groups respected.

Child protection and the law

We need to be mindful of pupils' safety at all times. The Children Act was drawn up to protect the welfare of the child and this was updated in 2004, supported by the publication of guidance called *Every Child Matters: Change for Children*.

Every Child Matters sets out a new approach to ensuring the well-being of children and young people aged 0–19. The Government's aim is for every child to have the support they need to:

○ be healthy
○ stay safe
○ enjoy and achieve
○ make a positive contribution
○ achieve economic well-being.

In order to achieve this, the legislation states that:

○ a children's commissioner will be appointed
○ there will be improved coordination between the agencies who deal with children – schools, social workers, the police and health professionals
○ there will be swifter and more effective help for children with special or additional needs and those 'at risk'
○ children and young people will have far more say about issues that affect them.

There are several things you can do to ensure that the pupils you deal with are kept safe.

○ Make sure you listen carefully if pupils confide in you.
○ Be careful in your questioning not to 'lead' them into telling you what has happened.
○ Keep notes of exactly what you have seen or been told. If you notice anything suspicious such as marks on a child you should:
  – never promise that you will not tell anyone else
  – pass on details of what they have told you immediately to your school's child protection officer (usually the headteacher).

- Do not discuss your initial concerns with the child's parents – seek advice from your SENCO and headteacher.
- Be careful if you are working on your own with children away from others – if you have to go into a room alone with a child, leave the door open or ajar.

For more information on child protection and pupils' safety see:

- www.teachernet.gov.uk/childprotection
- www.everychildmatters.gov.uk
- www.publications.doh.gov.uk/safeguardingchildren.

LIST 78 Health and safety in your work

The Health and Safety at Work Act 1974 was designed to protect everyone at work through procedures for preventing accidents and it applies in schools. Education employers have duties to ensure the health, welfare and safety of:

○ teachers and other education staff
○ pupils in school and on off-site visits
○ visitors to school and volunteers involved in school activities.

As an employee you also have responsibilities to:

○ take reasonable care of your own and others' safety
○ make sure your action doesn't harm others
○ cooperate with your employer
○ carry out activities in accordance with appropriate training and instruction
○ inform your employer of any serious risks.

As a teaching assistant you should:

○ make sure you have read and understood your school's health and safety policy
○ take action to minimize both internal and external hazards
○ ensure equipment is stored and moved safely
○ use appropriate safety equipment
○ dispose of waste safely
○ let others know where you are at all times
○ take appropriate action in an emergency (see also Chapter 9 Help!).

Data protection

The Data Protection Act is applicable to schools as they hold a great deal of information about pupils. It is important that any information held is stored securely, either password-protected on a computer or put in a locked cupboard. The Data Protection Act is:

○ designed to protect the information which is held by organizations from being abused by others
○ governed by eight principles of good practice which state that information must be:

  – fairly and lawfully processed
  – processed for limited purposes
  – adequate, relevant and not excessive
  – accurate and up to date
  – not kept longer than necessary
  – processed in accordance with the individual's rights
  – kept secure
  – not transferred to countries outside the European Economic Area.

As a teaching assistant you should:

○ make sure any information you have is kept secure and confidential
○ be particularly careful with records which are held on computers – do not leave the computer unattended when updating information.

For further information see www.informationcommissioner.gov.uk.

Restraining pupils

The Education Act section 550A allows adults to use 'reasonable force' to control or restrain pupils. Remember that the use of any degree of force is unlawful if the situation does not warrant it.

○ Restraint should only be used where action is necessary in self-defence or there is an imminent risk of injury or damage to property.
○ Before you intervene physically you must tell the pupil to stop and explain what will happen if they do not.
○ During intervention you must tell the pupil that the physical restraint will stop as soon as it ceases to be necessary.
○ Always remain calm.
○ Write a report of any incidents which occur and speak to your headteacher immediately.
○ Consult your school's policy for clarification.

Help! 9

LIST 81   Common safety issues

In schools, as in any other working environment, there will be areas of risk. It is up to all members of staff to be alert to hazards and minimize them where possible. These risks may result from:

- use and maintenance of equipment – broken furniture, poor storage, untidy working and learning environments, e.g. PE equipment, cooking areas, playground areas, science equipment
- use of materials and substances, e.g. in science lessons or during art and creative activities
- unsafe behaviour – pupils acting inappropriately
- accidental breakages and spillages – always clear these up or send for help immediately
- environmental factors, such as trailing wires, items left in corridors, obstructed fire doors, etc.
- animals or insects kept in school – these should always be fed and cleaned out regularly
- unauthorized or suspicious people in the learning environment – always report them immediately
- outdoor hazards, such as:
  - poisonous plants
  - animal mess
  - bins (overloaded or containing dangerous items)
  - ponds (should be fenced off and pupils should only visit when accompanied by an adult).

LIST 82

How to minimize risk

As a member of staff, you should be aware of precautions to be taken for your own health and safety and that of others.

- Be aware of the types of health and safety risks that may occur and regularly check your own working environment.
- Know your school's health and safety policy – you should have your own copy.
- Report hazards and label broken items.
- Use any safety equipment provided for lessons (round-ended scissors, gloves, goggles), store it correctly and teach pupils to do the same.
- Follow safety instructions on any equipment.
- Take action to minimize both internal and external hazards.
- Store materials correctly and move them carefully.
- Clean up spillages and breakages immediately or report them.
- Lock hazardous items away after use and tidy areas as you go.
- Ensure someone knows where you are at all times during school hours.
- Follow security procedures, e.g. signing in visitors and giving out badges.
- Take appropriate action in an emergency (See List 83, Emergencies).
- Know the identity and whereabouts of your school's health and safety officer.
- Know the identity and whereabouts of your school's first-aider.
- Make a note of the location of first-aid boxes.
- Check the location of emergency safety equipment and how to use it, including:
  - fire extinguishers (know about different types!)
  - fire blankets
  - fire exits and alarms.

L I S T 83 Emergencies

Hopefully you will never need to deal with any of these scenarios –
but be aware of them and what you would do. In all cases, send for
a first-aider immediately.

○ Severe bleeding – remove clothing around the wound. Lie the
pupil down and attempt to stem the flow by pressing hard down
on the wound.

○ Cardiac arrest – do not attempt cardio pulmonary resuscitation
(CPR) unless trained. Place the pupil in the recovery position if
they are unconscious (see List 85 The recovery position).

○ Shock – lie the pupil down, loosen clothing at the neck and keep
warm.

○ Fainting or loss of consciousness – sit the pupil down and put
their head between their knees. If they faint, lie them on their
back and raise their legs to increase blood flow. Loosen clothing
at the neck and keep the pupil quiet.

○ Epileptic seizure – do not restrain the pupil, but put something
soft beneath their head, if possible.

○ Choking and difficulty breathing – encourage the pupil to cough,
if possible. Bend them over with their head lower than their chest
and slap them between the shoulder blades to dislodge the
blockage.

○ Falls – treat all cases as actual fractures, even if you think
something is only potentially broken. Do not attempt to move
the pupil.

○ Burns and scalds – cool the affected area immediately with cold
water. Do not remove any clothes which are stuck to the burn.

○ Poisoning – find out what the pupil has swallowed and stay with
them, watching for signs of unconsciousness. Take the suspect
poison to hospital with you.

○ Electrocution – cut off the source of electricity immediately. If
this is not possible, move the pupil away from the source using
something wooden, such as a chair. Do not touch the pupil until
you have done this. Then place them in the recovery position (see
List 85).

○ Substance abuse – find out what has happened if possible. Place
the pupil in the recovery position if unconscious.

LIST 84 What to remember in an emergency

○ Call for assistance immediately but stay with the pupil.

○ Look for possible triggers, see if the pupil carries a medical alert card, and ask them, if possible.

○ Check DRABC (danger, response, airway, breathing, circulation).
  - are you or the pupil in danger?
  - can you get a response from them?
  - open the airway by tilting the pupil's head back slightly
  - look, listen and feel for breathing
  - look for signs of circulation, such as coughing, movement.

○ To assess the level of response, check AVPU (is the casualty alert, does he/she have a voice, are they in pain or unresponsive?).

○ Look for secondary conditions – problems with hearing, smell, head lumps/bumps, fluids, blood, broken bones.

○ Use the recovery position (see List 85).

○ Keep the pupil warm.

○ Loosen clothing or jewellery if necessary.

○ Think about any religious or cultural restrictions on the actions you take.

○ Remember that actions beyond your own capabilities can endanger life.

○ Remember potential health risks, e.g. wear gloves.

○ Provide verbal and physical support at all times.

○ Once help arrives:
  - continue to assist
  - make the vicinity private and safe
  - offer support to others involved.

○ Record and report the accident or emergency.

L I S T 85 **The recovery position**

Use the recovery position in an emergency situation if the pupil is breathing but has no other life-threatening conditions.

○ Kneel beside the pupil and turn their head towards you, lifting it back to open the airway.

○ Place their nearest arm straight down their side and the other arm across their chest. Place the far ankle over the near ankle.

○ While holding the head with one hand, hold the pupil at the hip by their clothing and turn them onto their front by pulling towards you, supporting them with your knees.

○ Lift the chin forward to keep the airway open.

○ Bend the arm and leg nearest to you, and pull out the other arm from under the body, palm up.

○ Check that they cannot roll forwards or backwards.

○ If the injuries allow, turn the pupil to the other side after 30 minutes.

LIST 86 Common medical conditions and illnesses

Always keep an eye out for signs that a pupil may be unwell, particularly if you notice they are not 'themselves'. Some illnesses have long incubation periods. Remember also that coughs and colds can also cause pupils to have restricted hearing.

○ Anaphylactic shock – most commonly caused by an extreme allergic reaction. Sit the pupil down and try to keep them calm. Send for a first-aider or someone trained to use an epipen, and call an ambulance.

○ Asthma – difficulty breathing. Keep the pupil calm and send for their inhaler if they have one in school. Failing this, call the parents or family doctor.

○ Chicken pox – patches of itchy red spots with white centres. The pupil should be kept off school for five days from the onset of the rash.

○ Conjunctivitis – inflammation of the membranes lining the eyelids. This is highly contagious and some schools prefer pupils not to attend until they are better.

○ Diabetes – lack of insulin which regulates blood sugar. Symptoms include loss of weight and strong thirst. If undiagnosed the first sign can be a diabetic coma.

○ Epilepsy – frequently begins in infancy. There are two types of epileptic fit, petit mal which is often compared with daydreaming, and grand mal in which the patient falls to the ground and shakes or twitches. Do not attempt to restrain a pupil, but put something soft under their head and wait for the fit to pass.

○ German measles – a pink rash on the head, trunk and limbs. Most infectious before diagnosis. The pupil should be kept off school for five days from the onset of the rash.

○ Measles – fever, with runny eyes, rash, sore throat and cough. Pupils need rest and plenty of fluids and should not be in school.

○ Mumps – a viral infection which includes a high temperature, muscle pains and swelling of the salivary glands, usually those in front of the ears. It can be infectious from 24 hours before the swelling appears until three days after it has gone down.

○ Tonsillitis – very sore throat, fever and inflamed tonsils. Pupils should be kept off school and may need antibiotics.

L I S T 87   Completing accident forms

By law, schools must always record and report accidents, whether major or minor. There may be a school accident book and/or a local authority accident form. Make sure you record the incident as soon as possible so that you don't forget any of the details. Information required will be:

○ name of pupil
○ date and time of accident
○ what happened and where
○ the cause of the accident
○ injuries that occurred
○ the treatment given
○ who administered the treatment.

This will be kept on the premises in case there needs to be any further inquiry into the incident.

Some schools also send accident slips out to parents if, for example, a child has had an accident and bumped their head. It is useful for the parents to know so that they can watch for symptoms of delayed concussion.

Administering medication and first-aid

Schools will usually have their own procedures for the storage and administering of medicines and you may be involved with this, particularly if you are a trained first-aider.

❍ Unless pupils have a medical condition where it is essential that medicines are kept in school, it is unlikely that parents will be encouraged to leave medication on school premises.

❍ Medication includes applying creams or lotions and using inhalers.

❍ If it is in school, medication should be kept in a safe place and should be clearly labelled.

❍ Medication should not be given to pupils without the written permission of parents or carers.

❍ In case of emergency, inhalers or epipens may also be kept in classrooms.

What to have in your first-aid box

❍ A leaflet giving general advice on first-aid.

❍ Several individually wrapped, sterile adhesive dressings of assorted sizes.

❍ Two sterile eye pads.

❍ Four individually wrapped triangular bandages.

❍ Six safety pins.

❍ Six medium-sized, individually wrapped, unmedicated wound dressings.

❍ Disposable gloves.

❍ Scissors.

Moving On | 10

Before applying

Wherever you are, at some point you will need to consider changing your job or gaining more qualifications. Even if you feel settled and enjoy what you are doing, it is always a good idea to keep looking for ways of extending yourself.

- ○ Remember, applying for a job is a two-way process: you are looking for a school and job for yourself and the school is looking for the ideal applicant.
- ○ Check the advertisement carefully to see whether you need additional qualifications or experience.
- ○ See if you need to fill in a form or write a covering letter with a CV.
- ○ Find out a bit about the school if you can – check its reputation, go and visit.
- ○ Make sure you do not fill in applications in a hurry or at the last minute – you will forget to include all details and won't present yourself in the best light.

Making an application

You will find that some job advertisements ask you to send in your curriculum vitae (CV), whereas others will have an application form you can send for to fill in. Whichever you use, make sure that you provide all the information that is required.

Writing a CV

○ Ensure you include all essential details:
- name, address
- contact details
- date of birth
- marital status and dependants
- qualifications
- employment history (starting with current employer)
- other interests, activities and experience, e.g. bee-keeping, rock-climbing.
○ Make sure you give information about:
- any training you have had, including any specific special educational needs training, ICT training, INSET
- responsibilities, e.g. running clubs, organizing trips
- experience, e.g. knowledge of specific special needs.
○ Keep and update your CV on an annual basis.

Application forms

○ Make sure you answer all the questions.
○ Keep your application as neat as possible.
○ Be totally truthful – an incorrect answer might result in a dismissal at a later date.
○ If you need to continue on another piece of paper, label it carefully.
○ Always ask referees for permission before using them and make sure you have their correct contact details.
○ Return your application by the specified date.

LIST 91

Writing a covering letter

You may need to add a covering letter if there is no application form or space for a supporting statement. Use it to sell yourself and explain why you think you are the right person for the post.

○ Check through the person specification and establish what they are looking for – make sure you include details about all the points highlighted.

○ Outline any previous experience that might be relevant.

○ Include training you have had, if this is not stated elsewhere.

○ Include areas of expertise, e.g. you might be able to run an out-of-school club if you are an expert in music.

○ Ask someone else to read through and check it for you – you may not always notice errors yourself.

LIST 92   Going to interviews

○ Make sure you arrive in good time.
○ Dress comfortably but sensibly:
  - do not wear t-shirts with large logos or slogans
  - skirts should not be too short or suits too loud
  - better to be conservative than to try to make a fashion statement!
○ Think about the interview the night before and be prepared (see List 93 Common interview questions). Have one or two questions to ask the panel at the end of the interview.
○ Look calm – get settled and try not to look anxious, even if you are!
○ Put bags and coats out of the way before you start.
○ Make eye contact with those running the interview.
○ Smile! It will put everyone at ease if you can use a little humour.
○ Try to relax – remember that the people giving the interview are often nervous too!
○ Make sure you find out before leaving how and when you will be notified if you are successful.
○ At the end of the interview, smile and thank your interviewers.
○ Remember that you are choosing to work at the school – you do not have to work there if you are not happy with the school or what is asked of you.

LIST 93

Common interview questions

It's best to be prepared for some of the questions you will be asked at interview. Think about some of these and how you would answer them.

- ○ Why have you applied for the post?
- ○ What experience have you had with ... ?
- ○ What sort of training have you had?
- ○ What difficulties have you had in the past and how have you coped with them?
- ○ How do you see the role of the teaching/support assistant?
- ○ What would you do in the following situations ... ?
- ○ What would you do if a parent came to you with a question about their child?
- ○ What would you do to make the pupil as independent as possible?
- ○ What would you do if a task set was too difficult for the pupil?
- ○ What would you do if a pupil rushed through their work and then said they had finished?
- ○ What are your views on discipline?
- ○ What challenges do you think a pupil with dyslexia/autism/ ADHD could face in a mainstream classroom?
- ○ Have you any first-aid qualifications or experience?

Coping with questions

○ Do not try to answer all questions straight away – think about each answer briefly before you give it.

○ Listen carefully to what is being asked.

○ Look at the person who is asking the question.

○ Ask for clarification if you do not understand the question.

○ Answer questions honestly. If you don't know the answer, say so. It will be easy to know if you are not telling the truth.

○ Sit upright and look interested. Try not to move around or fidget too much.

○ Be wary of any questions which ask you about ethnicity, sexual orientation or childcare arrangements – you do not have to answer these.

LIST 95

Questions to ask at interview

You should have a few questions up your sleeve to ask the panel at the end of the interview and they should give you the opportunity to do this. If they don't, ask them! This will show initiative, which is what they are looking for in a teaching assistant. Here are some ideas for things you could ask.

○ Are teaching assistants given any planning time with teachers?
○ Are we able to make suggestions for activities with pupils?
○ Will I be able to go on any courses?
○ Does the school hold regular meetings for assistants?
○ Will I be able to change year groups or subject areas from year to year?
○ Can I say which year group I would prefer to work with?
○ If I support a child with special educational needs, will the school make sure I am fully trained?
○ I can play the guitar/recorder/coach netball/rugby – would I be able to run a club?
○ Would it be possible to have a tour of the school?

What you should not ask:

○ Why do teachers get paid so much more than teaching assistants?
○ Why don't I get paid for the holidays?
○ Can I have days off during term time?
○ Do I have to go on school trips?

Remember that you are trying to present yourself in the best light and by asking questions which suggest the school is not being flexible enough you will not be helping yourself.

Observations and inspections

You will almost certainly at some point be part of a school which is being inspected by Ofsted and it is likely that during this process you will be observed in the classroom working with children. You may also be observed as part of a college course or HLTA training.

○ Make sure you are clear about what the teacher wants you to do well before the session begins.
○ If your observation is part of a college course, make sure in advance the school and individual teachers know that your tutor is coming.
○ Ensure that you are well prepared and have all the resources you need.
○ Be prepared to answer questions about what you are doing or have done with pupils.
○ Remember, nobody is trying to 'catch you out'.
○ Relax and be yourself.

LIST 97 Appraisals

Annual appraisal is a process which is now undertaken in most professions and is increasingly being applied to teaching assistants. It is designed to monitor your professional development.

○ You will be interviewed about your role in the school and whether you feel your job description is still appropriate (see appraisal questions below).

○ You may be observed in the classroom by your line manager or headteacher.

○ You will be given the opportunity to make suggestions about how you would like to develop your role or training you feel you need.

○ It is a good opportunity for discussing issues which might not otherwise come to light.

○ You should look on an appraisal as a positive experience!

Common appraisal questions

Think about these before attending your appraisal interview as they could form the basis of your discussion:

○ Do you feel that your job description is still appropriate? Are there any changes which need to be made?

○ What targets were you set at your last appraisal or when you started your job? Have these been achieved? If not, why not?

○ What aspect of your job satisfies you the most?

○ What aspect of your job has not been as successful as you had anticipated?

○ Are there any aspects of your work which you would like to improve?

○ What training have you received? Has it been successful?

○ What are your current training needs?

Career development

- Keep up to date with recent developments for teaching assistants through reading publications such as *The Times Educational Supplement*.
- Make sure you attend as much training as you can.
- Join a union, as they will send you regular newsletters and information.
- Be prepared to gain a qualification – teaching assistant salaries may be linked to this in the near future.
- Find out about teaching assistants in other schools and what is available to them.
- Shadow other assistants wherever possible to gain new ideas.
- Make the most of any opportunities you can to gain further experience.

L I S T 99 **Going back to college**

It is likely that during the next few years, schools will start to ask for assistants to have qualifications for the work that they do. Increasingly, jobs advertised will ask for NVQs or Higher Level Teaching Assistants. If you do decide to get a qualification as a teaching assistant, there a few points to remember.

○ Investigate all your local colleges to see which qualifications they offer and make sure you are clear on what they mean (see also List 6 Duties and qualifications).
○ Call or go to the college to find out more if necessary.
○ Compare issues such as:
  – cost
  – any entry requirements
  – interviews and assessments required
  – length of course
  – validity of qualification
  – time spent in college and in the workplace
  – whether you will be assessed in school as well as through written work.
○ Make sure you check with your school or local education authority to see what courses you may be entitled to attend. Ask the LEA whether your qualification will entitle you to a salary increase!
○ Update your English and mathematics skills if necessary – you may not have to pay and it will enhance your work in the classroom. It is also necessary to have GCSE equivalents in these subjects if you are thinking of applying for HLTA status.
○ Don't worry! Many adults go back to college and education later in life and you will find that you are not the only person who is returning to learning.
○ Socialize! A big plus point will be meeting TAs from other schools and sharing your experiences.
○ Involve yourself in your college as much as you can: make use of the library, support services, guidance and any help you can obtain with fees or childcare costs.

Juggling home, work and study

Don't be put off by the idea of trying to combine work, study and home life – many others have done it before you! It can seem daunting if you have a family, but most teaching assistant courses are part time and many schools will allow some time out of the classroom to gain a qualification.

- You will find that others on your course will support you through studying together or sharing ideas.
- Speak to your family about what you are doing and ask everyone to help with the chores.
- Plan your use of time so that you allocate a certain number of hours each week to family, study, housework, etc.
- If you have children, send them to a friend one afternoon each week and then have their children back to give each of you more time.
- Make sure you have some 'you' time each week, even if this is just for a couple of hours – give yourself something to look forward to.
- Enjoy the great sense of achievement when you have completed your qualification!

LIST 101 **Useful websites**

You will find masses of information about working in schools on the Internet. Check out some of these websites as a starting point:

- www.dfes.gov.uk
- www.tda.gov.uk (go to 'support staff')
- www.teachernet.gov.uk
- www.tes.co.uk
- www.hlta.gov.uk
- www.lg-employers.gov.uk
- www.literacymatters.co.uk/hlta.html
- www.dyslexia-inst.org.uk/tadates.html
- www.bda-dyslexia.org.uk
- www.becta.org.uk
- www.curriculumonline.gov.uk
- www.ofsted.gov.uk
- www.tasonlinemagazine.org
- www.bbc.co.uk/schools
- www.standards.dfes.gov.uk/keystage3
- www.skills4schools.co.uk
- www.learningsupport.co.uk
- www.classroom-assistant.net
- www.teaching-assistants.co.uk